SUPER SPORTS ★ STAR

DEREK JETER

Ken Rappoport

Enslow Publishers, Inc.

40 Industrial Road   PO Box 38
Box 398   Aldershot
Berkeley Heights, NJ 07922   Hants GU12 6BP
USA   UK

http://www.enslow.com

Library of Congress Cataloging-in-Publication Data

Rappoport, Ken.
    Super sports star Derek Jeter / Ken Rappoport.
      p. cm. — (Super sports star)
    Summary: Discusses the personal life and baseball career of the star
    shortstop for the New York Yankees, Derek Jeter.
    Includes bibliographical references and index.
    ISBN 0-7660-2139-4
    1. Jeter, Derek, 1974– —Juvenile literature. 2. Baseball players—United
States—Biography—Juvenile literature. [1. Jeter, Derek, 1974– 2. Baseball
players. 3. Racially mixed people—Biography.]
    I. Title. II. Series.
    GV865.J48R36 2004
    796.357'092—dc21   2003011290

Printed in the United States of America

10 9 8 7 6 5 4 3 2 1

To Our Readers:
We have done our best to make sure all Internet Addresses in this book were
active and appropriate when we went to press. However, the author and the
publisher have no control over and assume no liability for the material available
on those Internet sites or on other Web sites they may link to. Any comments or
suggestions can be sent by e-mail to comments@enslow.com or to the address on
the back cover.

Photo Credits: © 2002 Robert Beck/MLB Photos, pp. 1, 34; © 2002
Grieshop/MLB Photos, pp. 29, 36; © 2001 Allen Kee/MLB Photos, p. 20;
© 2002 MLB Photos, p. 14; © Rich Pilling/MLB Photos, p. 31; © 2001 Rich
Pilling/MLB Photos, pp. 6, 13, 26, 42; © 2002 Rich Pilling/MLB Photos,
pp. 4, 10, 16, 23, 39, 45.

Cover Photo: © 2002 Robert Beck/MLB Photos

CONTENTS

4

Introduction

Derek Jeter is a special baseball player. He stands out in every part of the game. He hits for power and is a great base runner. He is a slick fielder and has a powerful arm. Above all, Jeter is a winner.

He jumped right to the top in his very first season as the New York Yankees' starting shortstop. In 1996, he helped the Yankees win their first World Series in eighteen years. By the age of twenty-four, he had already played on four World Series winners.

He has won many personal awards. In 2000, he was named the Most Valuable Player in the All-Star game. He also won MVP honors in the World Series the same year. That was a first for any player.

Whether hitting home runs, dashing around the bases, or making great plays on the field, Derek Jeter is a dazzling player.

All-Star Hero

It was the 2000 season. Derek Jeter was excited about his first start in the All-Star game. He was also nervous.

Jeter had not expected to start for the American League. Alex Rodriguez of the Texas Rangers had been selected by the fans. But he was injured. American League manager Joe Torre selected Jeter to take his place.

Not everybody liked the idea. Some said Torre only picked Jeter because he was one of his own players on the New York Yankees. Many felt there were other shortstops that deserved the honor.

Jeter was not concerned with what people said. He just wanted to do his best. But in previous All-Star appearances, Jeter had not exactly looked like an all-star. Two games, two times at bat, two strikeouts. Could he do better this time?

On the mound for the National League was Randy Johnson. He was one of the hardest throwers in baseball. He led the league in strikeouts many times. Jeter did not want to strike out again as he did in previous All-Star games. He hoped he was due for a hit.

In his first at bat he went up swinging hard. He cracked the ball into the outfield. Double! Jeter had his first All-Star hit.

In the third inning, Jeter singled off Kevin Brown. He then scored the American League's first run.

When Jeter came to the plate in the fourth inning, the score was tied, 1–1. On the mound for the National League was Al Leiter. Once again, Jeter went up swinging hard. This time, he hit another single. Two runs scored. The American League led, 3–1, and was on its way to a 6–3 victory.

In three times at bat against the National League's best pitchers, the Yankee shortstop had three hits. He drove in two runs, scored another, and won the Most Valuable Player award. It was a first for a Yankee player.

Derek Jeter showed why he was known as a player who always came through with timely hits. It had been that way ever since he was a high school star in Kalamazoo, Michigan.

Born to be a Yankee

As a young boy, it was Jeter's dream to play shortstop for the Yankees. His dream had come true.

Derek woke up early to play every day. "All his cousins would be sleeping, and he would say, 'C'mon, Gram, let's throw,'" his grandmother said. "He wanted to be a pitcher then. I was his catcher. Even as a little kid his throw would knock me over."

Derek's grandmother loved the Yankees. She took him to games. Before long, he was a big fan. His blue Yankee windbreaker was his favorite jacket. He also owned a gold Yankees medallion. His favorite player was Dave Winfield. Someday, he hoped to be just like his hero.

"Kids I went to school with used to laugh when I told them I wanted to play major league baseball," Jeter said. "People said that no one from Kalamazoo had played in the majors, so I couldn't do it."

But while growing up in the Michigan town, Derek thought otherwise. Derek's father gave him baseball lessons. Charles Jeter was a baseball player himself in college. "I practiced at it every day," Jeter said. "As far as I can remember, I was always in baseball."

Very often that meant playing with his sister, Sharlee, and mother, Dot. "My mom and sister would be in the outfield and would flag down all the balls I would hit," Jeter said.

In Little League, Derek played three infield positions. He was a shortstop, second baseman, and third baseman. His father coached him. Derek learned from both his parents to work hard and respect others.

Derek was born in Pequannock, New Jersey,

Derek Jeter dreamed of playing for the Yankees as a little boy.

Derek Jeter
swings at the
ball for a hit.

on June 26, 1974. His father is black and from Alabama. His mother is white and from New Jersey. When Derek was four, the family moved to Kalamazoo, Michigan. His father had a job there as a school counselor. Derek liked to spend his summers in New Jersey with his grandmother. He went to games at Yankee Stadium. He played baseball from dawn to dusk.

CHAPTER

3

Good Field, Good Hit

In high school, Derek was the hardest worker on his team. "He was the last one off the field every night," coach Don Zomer said. "He loves the game of baseball."

A buzz went through the crowd as the team took the field. The stands were packed. Everyone was there to see Derek Jeter. In his senior year in high school he was the star attraction.

Several major-league scouts were watching. They came from all over the country to see Derek play. They were amazed.

"Even his outs were impressive," Zomer said. "Derek hit balls normal high school players just couldn't handle."

In his senior year he led his team with a .508 batting average. That means he had at least one hit every two times at bat.

Derek was named the National High School Player of the Year in 1992. He was not only tops in baseball. He was also among the top students in his class. Derek was an honor student with a 3.82 grade average.

He accepted a baseball scholarship from the University of Michigan. Then he waited to see what happened in the baseball draft. Teams take turns picking the best players out of high school and college. Derek hoped to be picked by his favorite team, the New York Yankees.

On draft day, the phone rang in Derek's house. He held his breath. It was the Yankees. They had selected him in the first round of the draft. He was the first high school player picked by the major-league teams. Derek was thrilled, but he also wanted to play college ball. The Yankees helped make up his mind.

"Education is a big thing in our family," Derek said. "Signing with the Yankees was no easy decision because I really wanted to go to school and play baseball at Michigan. But I couldn't say no when they were paying for college, too."

Derek picked up a seven hundred thousand dollar bonus just for signing a contract. He was only eighteen years old and heading for pro ball. But there were some hard times ahead for him.

CHAPTER
4

Up the Minor-League Ladder

Derek Jeter was not hitting. He was making errors. He was playing in the Gulf Coast rookie league in Tampa, Florida. He was far from home and missed his friends and family. He was very unhappy.

"That first year was rough," Jeter said. "That was the first time I was ever away from home, and I was terrible. Two and a half months seemed like forever to me." Jeter thought he had made a mistake by signing with the Yankees. "You start thinking, 'Were you ready? Should you have gone to college?'"

Next stop for Jeter was the Greensboro Hornets. The Hornets played in the South Atlantic League. It was the first step up from the rookie league. It was still a long way from the major leagues.

At Greensboro, Jeter improved his batting. But he was still having trouble in the field. He made error after error at shortstop. That was not the only thing that was bothering him.

"I was homesick," Derek Jeter said. "When they told me at Tampa that I was coming [to Greensboro], I should have been happy to move up. But I just wanted to go home."

In 1993, Jeter made 56 errors. That was the second highest by a shortstop in his league. But he was not a quitter. Just like in high school, he worked hard. He improved his defense. One national baseball magazine named Derek Jeter its best minor league defensive shortstop.

Now it was the 1994 season. Jeter was feeling better about his chances of doing well in pro ball. He played in the Class-A level in Tampa, Florida. Then he played in the Class-AA level in Albany, New York. Finally the Yankees promoted Jeter to their top minor-league team in Columbus, Ohio. This was Class AAA. He was one step away from the big leagues.

Jeter's strong play in the minor leagues helped him make it to the Yankees.

It was a hot August day. Jeter stepped up to the plate for the Columbus Clippers for the first time. He set himself in the batter's box. In came the pitch. He swung. Double! He singled later in the game. The Clippers beat Scranton-Wilkes Barre, 3–2.

"I wanted to get off to a good start," Jeter said.

One week later Jeter smashed three hits. He showed good power with a home run. He drove in three runs. He scored two, and he stole a base. Columbus beat Toledo, 9–7, in 10 innings. It was only Jeter's seventh game at the Triple-A level.

Jeter had an outstanding season. Playing for three teams, he hit a total of 7 home runs and knocked in 68. He also stole 50 bases. His batting average of .344 was one of the best in the minors. He was just as proud of his improved fielding. In 616 chances he had only made 25 errors. Jeter was named Minor League Player of the Year. Only one thing could top that as far as he was concerned: playing for the New York Yankees.

Was he ready to make the jump to the major leagues?

Rookie Sensation

The loudspeaker blared, "Playing shortstop for the New York Yankees—Derek Jeter." When he was a kid, Jeter used to imagine that someday he would hear his name announced like that at Yankee Stadium. Now it was happening.

"I went out on the field and looked around and it was like, 'Am I really here?'" Jeter said.

It was the summer of 1995. Yankee shortstop Tony Fernandez was hurt. The Yankees brought Jeter up from the minors. He played fifteen games.

The following year, Jeter was named starting shortstop for the Yankees on Opening Day. Jeter was nervous. He knew it would not be easy. New York baseball fans demanded the best from their players.

Jeter got off to a good start. In his very first game, he hit a home run against Cleveland.

The Yankees beat the Indians, 7–1. Jeter did not let up. By the end of the season, he had a .314 batting average. He scored 104 runs and drove in 78. He sparked the Yankees into the playoffs.

In the postseason, he continued to hit the ball hard. His mighty .412 batting average helped the Yankees knock out Texas in the first round. Then the battle for the American League title opened in New York. The Yankees faced Baltimore. They hoped to get the jump on the Orioles at home. Baltimore was leading, 4–3, in the eighth inning when Jeter came up to hit.

He hit a long drive to right field. Home run! The score was tied. Then in the 11th inning, Bernie Williams homered. The Yankees won, 5–4. The Yankees kept winning. Jeter provided the spark with a key homer and a .417 batting average against the Orioles.

Derek Jeter
helped the
Yankees
beat the
Braves to
win the
World Series
in 1996.

Now it was World Series time. The Yankees faced Atlanta. The Braves won the first two games in New York. Things looked bad for the Yankees. The Series moved to Atlanta. The Yankees needed to win at least two of the three games to have a chance. They won all three. Now the teams were back at Yankee Stadium. The Yankees could clinch the Series in Game 6. Jeter drove in a run. His hit sparked a three-run rally. The Yankees beat the Braves, 3–2. It was their first world championship since 1978.

Derek Jeter was later given another prize. He was named Rookie of the Year.

"It was just an incredible year," Jeter said.

Rising to the Occasion

Derek Jeter was worried. It was the 1997 season and there was trouble. He was striking out. His batting average had dropped.

"I've made a lot of mistakes," he said during the year. "Part of the problem is that I'm trying to prove last year wasn't a fluke, and I try too hard."

The season ended too quickly for Jeter and the Yankees. They were knocked out of the playoffs. They missed their chance to become world champions again.

Could they make a comeback in 1998? The Yankees came to spring training camp with just that in mind. They worked hard. They were going to show the baseball world that they were the best team.

By May, the Yankees were in first place.

On May 18, they had the top record in baseball at 28–9. It was the best start by a Yankee team since 1928. Jeter was hot. He was hitting .337. That was one of the best batting averages in the league. He paced the Yankees with 10 steals.

Day by day the victories piled up. When the regular season ended, the Yankees had won an amazing 114 games. It was the best record in American League history. Jeter played a big role. He nearly doubled his home run total of the previous season. He boosted his batting average and RBIs to career bests. The Yankees were back in the playoffs for the third straight year.

No less than a World Series title would satisfy them. They rolled through the postseason. In the Series, they met the San Diego Padres. The Yankees opened with two victories at Yankee Stadium. They flew west to play the next two games in San Diego. Another Yankee victory in Game 3. New York was one victory away from the world championship.

A crowd of 65,427 filled Qualcomm

Derek Jeter helped his team win more games in one season than any other team in major league history.

Stadium in San Diego. The fans saw a great pitchers' duel. It was the Yankees' Andy Pettitte against the Padres' Kevin Brown. After five innings, the teams were scoreless.

Then in the sixth, Jeter beat out an infield hit. Paul O'Neill followed with a double sending Jeter to third. Bernie Williams hit a chopper to the mound. Jeter got a good jump and raced home with the game's first run. It was the start of a three-run rally. The Yankees were on their way to a 3–0 victory. They were world champions.

What a season for the Yankees and Derek Jeter. The Yankees won 125 games counting the regular season and playoffs. That was more than any team in baseball history. They had made their case as the best team ever. And Jeter had made his case as one of baseball's best players.

CHAPTER 7

Dashing Derek

Good hitter. Good fielder. Good guy. That is what people say about Derek Jeter.

Jeter is one of the nicest people in baseball. He makes time to help people. He was given an award for community service. He visits sick children in hospitals. His Turn 2 Foundation helps teenagers stay away from alcohol and drugs. At the ballpark he tries to sign as many autographs as he can. The fans love Derek Jeter. And he loves them back.

"New York has the best fans in any sport," Jeter says.

In 1999, the Yankees were back in the World Series. Jeter had just finished his greatest season. He batted .349 with 24 home runs. He scored 134 runs and drove in 102. In the playoffs, he hit safely in every game. He helped the Yankees beat Atlanta for the title.

Jeter showed he was a player who thrived

under great pressure. He extended his postseason hitting streak to 17 games. It was a major-league record. "If this is a dream don't wake me up," Jeter said.

Were there more titles to come? The New York Mets had other ideas. As champions of the National League, the Mets faced the American League champion Yankees in the 2000 World Series. The so-called "Subway Series" sparked excitement all over New York. It was the first time the Mets and Yankees had met in the World Series.

After three games, the Yankees held a 2–1 lead. Each game was a thriller. At Shea Stadium for Game 4, the Mets could have tied the Series with a win. Derek Jeter stepped into the batter's box to lead off. He lashed the first pitch. Home run! In his next at bat, he tripled and then he scored. The Yankees were off to a 3–2 victory.

On the following night, the Yankees fell behind the Mets. But Jeter hit a home run.

Derek Jeter
helped the
Yankees beat
the Mets in the
first Subway
Series between
those teams.

Tie game! The shot sparked the Yankees to a 4–2 victory and another world championship. During the season, Jeter had been the Most Valuable Player at the All-Star game. Now he was also World Series MVP.

In 2001, the Yankees made the playoffs again. They faced Oakland in the first round. The Yankees were leading, 1–0, in the seventh inning of game four. But the A's had a runner on base. The batter hit a drive down the right field line. A's runner Jason Giambi raced around third base. He headed for home. The throw came in from the outfield. It looked like Giambi would beat it and tie the game.

Suddenly Derek Jeter came out of nowhere. He had raced across the infield from his shortstop position to grab the relay throw. In one motion, he flipped the ball sidearm from foul territory to catcher Jorge Posada. Out! The run was saved. And so was the game.

"I was watching the right fielder and the runner," Yankees general manager Brian

Cashman said. "But then here came Derek Jeter to save the day."

The Yankees soon moved on to the next round and then into the World Series. Although they did not win the Series, Jeter was a star for the Yankees.

Through his career, Jeter had stayed free of serious injury. Early in the 2003 season, Jeter took a headfirst slide into third base against Toronto. He dislocated his left shoulder. No one knew how long he would be lost to the Yankees.

Jeter went into "rehab." That is when players do exercises to get better. He was out of action for more than a month. Finally, the injury healed well enough for him to play baseball again. The Yankees sent him to the minors to get sharp. He played a few games before returning to Yankee Stadium in May. He looked great at bat and in the field.

When Jeter came back to the Yankees, everyone was happy to see him. Jeter faced the Anaheim Angels in his first appearance after six

Derek Jeter was a star for his fielding in the 2001 playoffs.

weeks on the injury list. Base hit. He was back in form.

In June 2003 Jeter received a special honor. He was named the Yankees' captain—just the 11th in team history.

With Jeter leading the way, the Yankees won yet another American League pennant. There was no world championship this time, but Jeter's record had been amazing. In his first eight full years in the majors he had played on eight post-season teams, six pennant winners and four world champions.

As a boy, Derek Jeter had dreamed of playing for the Yankees. He idolized all the Yankee players. And now he could count himself among the all-time Yankee greats.

CAREER STATISTICS

											MLB	
Year	**Team**	**G**	**AB**	**R**	**H**	**2B**	**3B**	**HR**	**RBI**	**BB**	**SB**	**Avg.**
1995	NYY	15	48	5	12	4	1	0	7	3	0	.250
1996	NYY	157	582	104	183	25	6	10	78	48	14	.314
1997	NYY	159	654	116	190	31	7	10	70	74	23	.291
1998	NYY	149	626	127	203	25	8	19	84	57	30	.324
1999	NYY	158	627	134	219	37	9	24	102	91	19	.349
2000	NYY	148	593	119	201	31	4	15	73	68	22	.339
2001	NYY	150	614	110	191	35	3	21	74	56	27	.311
2002	NYY	157	644	124	191	26	0	18	75	73	32	.297
2003	NYY	119	482	87	156	25	3	10	52	43	11	.324
Total		**1,212**	**4,870**	**926**	**1,546**	**239**	**41**	**127**	**615**	**513**	**178**	**.317**

G—Games
AB—At Bats
R—Runs
H—Hits
2B—Doubles
3B—Triples

HR—Home Runs
RBI—Runs Batted In
BB—Bases on Balls (Walks)
SB—Stolen Bases
Avg.—Batting Average

Where to Write to Derek Jeter

Mr. Derek Jeter
c/o The New York Yankees
Yankee Stadium
44 E. 161st Street
Bronx, NY 10452

Derek Jeter continues his career as a great Yankee baseball player.

WORDS TO KNOW

All-Star Game—The midsummer classic matches the best players in the American and National Leagues.

major leagues—The top professional league in baseball. The majors include the American and National Leagues.

minor leagues—The minors are made up of all the other professional leagues. The players hope to some day play in the major leagues.

Most Valuable Player (MVP)—The award is given each year to the best player in the league. It is also handed out to the best player in the annual All-Star game.

rookie—A player in his first full season in professional sports.

scholarship—An award that allows a player to attend college for free.

shortstop—Part of the "middle infield" with the second baseman. The shortstop usually has the best range and strongest arm of all the infielders.

World Series—Each fall the champions of the American and National Leagues battle for the World Series title.

READING ABOUT

Books

Covert, Kim. *Derek Jeter*. Minnetonka, Minn.: Capstone Press, Inc., 2001.

Emerson, Carl. *Derek Jeter*. Eden Prairie, Minn.: The Child's World, Inc., 2001.

Fischer, David. *The Story of the New York Yankees*. New York, N.Y.: Dorling Kindersley Publishing, Inc., 2003.

January, Brendan. *Derek Jeter: Shortstop Sensation*. Danbury, Conn.: Scholastic Library Publishing, 2000.

Internet Addresses

The Official Web Site of the New York Yankees
<http://www.yankees.com/>

The Official Web Site of Major League Baseball
<http://mlb.com>

INDEX